It Started with Nails

by Karl Juergens

Illustrated by Tom Graham

PEARSON

Scott
Foresman

Editorial Offices: Glenview, Illinois • Parsippany, New Jersey • New York, New York
Sales Offices: Needham, Massachusetts • Duluth, Georgia • Glenview, Illinois
Coppell, Texas • Sacramento, California • Mesa, Arizona

Johannes wanted to be a carpenter. But he did not have any wood. He did not have a hammer or a saw. He only had nails.

Where can I find the things I need? Johannes wondered. Then he remembered. The marketplace would have those things!

In the marketplace, Johannes saw a merchant selling wood.

"I want to be a carpenter," Johannes said to the merchant. "I have nails. But I need some wood."

"I need nails to fix my sign," the merchant said. "If you'll fix my sign, I'll give you some wood." Johannes fixed the sign and took a wagon of wood.

sign

In the next stall, Johannes saw another merchant. She was selling hammers.

"I want to be a carpenter," Johannes told the second merchant. "I have wood and nails. Now I need a hammer."

"My roof is broken," the merchant said. "If you fix my roof, I will give you a hammer."

---

stall: a booth or a counter with things for sale

Johannes agreed to fix the roof. The merchant gave him a hammer and some safety **gear**. Johannes used the hammer, some of his nails, and some of his wood to fix the hole. The happy merchant told Johannes to keep the hammer and the safety gear.

---

gear: material used for an activity

Johannes continued to walk. He saw a merchant selling saws.

"I want to be a carpenter," he told the third merchant. "I have nails. I have some wood. I have a hammer. I have safety gear. Now I need a saw."

saws

"I need another shelf," the merchant told Johannes. "If you make a shelf for me, I will give you a saw."

The merchant handed Johannes a saw. Johannes cut some of his wood. He used his hammer and some nails to make the shelf.

The merchant was pleased. "Keep the saw!" he told Johannes.

safety mask

shelf

The next day, Johannes went to the marketplace. He carried his nails, his wood, his hammer, his saw, and his safety gear.

"I will build my own stall," he said. He cut the wood with the saw. He hammered the nails into the wood. When the stall was done, he hung out a sign that said: *Carpenter.*

"Now I am a carpenter!" he said.